Newlywed Book of Prayers

Praying for Your New Spouse

The Husband's Version

Doreen Wennberg

Fruit of the Vine Publishing

Newlywed Book of Prayers

Praying for your New Spouse

The Husband's Version

Copyright © 2017 by Doreen Wennberg

ISBN: 10: 0999590510

ISBN:13: 978-0-9995905-1-5

Fruit of the Vine Publishing

This book is dedicated to our newly married son and his wife and to all newlywed couples who desire to begin their lives with a Christ centered marriage. May God bless you and grant you intimacy with Him as you seek Him for one another.

It is my prayer that you will grow in your faith, in your dependence on the Lord, and in your relationship with your spouse.

~Doreen Wennberg

Newlywed Book of Prayers

CONTENTS

Newlywed Book of Prayers

Introduction

You promised to love, honor, and cherish one another, but pray? Did you promise to do that? The best strategy to keep harmony in your marriage with your wife is prayer. Still, some find these uncharted waters a bit overwhelming - after all, there are many areas to cover in prayer. For those who grew up with family devotions and prayers, this is all familiar. For those who did not grow up in an atmosphere of spiritual disciplines, this new concept may seem somewhat strange to you. All spiritual disciplines can seem unfamiliar at first. They are however, the key to developing a closer relationship between you and God and each other. Whether you pray on your own or together is not the issue. The point is, praying for your wife will inevitably draw you both closer to each other.

The biblical husband and wife relationship is designed to be God – centered. Every newlywed couple has the opportunity to start their new life off with God as the foundation and center of their marriage. If this is your desire as a couple and for your future children, prayer will be the key. Prayer is one of the most important things you can do to strengthen your bond.

This book is designed to help you to form a foundation of prayer for your marriage. People sometimes make the mistake of trying to get along with a spouse apart from God, and one can do that for a time, but marriages apart from God don't last very long. Perhaps you have already taken this leadership, if so wonderful. But if you haven't and are not yet comfortable in leading, you can use this booklet as a tool to pray on your own for your wife. In time, you'll want to share this with her. For a wife, a genuine prayer from a husbands heart can make her feel deeply loved. If it is your desire to have a long lasting and satisfying marriage, God will honor your prayers. When we leave God's work to Him, and ask in prayer, He is faithful to bring about the desires of our heart.

~Doreen Wennberg

About this Book

The benefit of selected scriptures and sample written prayers help us to learn or emulate prayer conversationally. As you pray, God will stir your own heart to the needs and situations personal to you.

Starting with the home—the place that will become the sanctuary for the couple away from the outside world. This chapter focuses on creating a tranquil environment, love for God, and one another.

Chapter 2 - Teaches praying for a strong marriage and the mutual aspects of love and respect.

Chapter 3 - The breakdown of communication in marriage happens all too often. Prayers anchored with scripture guide correct communication for a couple.

Chapter 4 - This chapter will arm the husband with scriptures for choosing like-minded friendships.

Chapter 5 - For God to be at the center of every marriage, church worship must be a priority.

Chapter 6 - The desire for most every couple is to have offspring. This chapter shows praying for our children begins before they are born.

Chapter 7 - Discipline in the study and reading of God's Word is difficult in today's demanding schedules. This chapter aids a husband with scriptures and prayers for a busy woman.

Chapter 8 - A wise man prays for his wife to fill her mind and heart with God's Word so others see His influence in her.

Chapter 9 - This chapter helps a husband to pray for God's purpose to be fulfilled in his wife's work.

Chapter 10 - A husband is his wife's covering—his prayers are her protection.

Chapter 11 - There are many ways a woman can be tempted. Through scripture and prayer a husband can help to guard his wife from falling.

Chapter 12 - This chapter aids a husband in praying for his wife to stay true to God, herself, and her husband.

1 Our Home

May our home be a place of peace where love resides; a house of prayer that reflects our faith and love for God.

The LORD blesses his people with peace. ~ Psalm 29:11b

Lord, I pray that You will bless our home with peace. I pray that you will increase our love for Your Word because Your Word says that they that love Your law have great peace. (Psalm 119:165)

Make me a tool for peace in our home. Use me to promote harmony and not strife. I pray for my wife to be a woman of quiet strength, one who seeks unity and pursues peace. May all who enter our home sense a tranquil environment because of Your presence that resides here. ~ In Jesus' Name.

Let us therefore make every effort to do what leads to peace and to mutual edification. ~ Romans 14:19

Turn from evil and do good; seek peace and pursue it. ~Ps. 34:14

Make every effort to keep the unity of the Spirit through the bond of peace. ~ Ephesians 4:3

Love in our home

And so we know and rely on the love God has for us. God is love. Whoever lives in love lives in God, and God in them. ~1 John 4:16

Lord, I pray that You increase our love for You and also for one another. I pray that we daily experience Your great love for us. I pray my wife knows and understand the depths of your love for Her. May we both continue to grow and walk in Your love. May Your love carry us through the difficult times. May Your love cause in us a kindness of heart. Make us thoughtful and caring toward one another. May we both love You with all of our heart, soul and mind. ~ In Jesus' Name.

I have loved you with an everlasting love; I have drawn you with loving – kindness. ~ Jeremiah 31:3

Above all, love each other deeply, because love covers over a multitude of sins. ~ 1Peter 4:8

Jesus replied: "Love the Lord your God with all your heart and with all your soul and with all your mind." ~ Matthew 22:37

Prayer in our home

They all joined together constantly in prayer. ~ Acts 1:14a

Lord, I pray that our home will become a place of prayer. I pray that we grow in the understanding of depending on You, and casting our worries and cares on You. May every problem that arises, cause us to turn to You in prayer. I pray that through crying out to You, we will experience Your faithfulness and peace. I pray that You will lead me to lead my wife and our children in prayer as the head of the home. ~ In Jesus' Name.

Do not be anxious about anything, but in every situation, by prayer and petition, with thanksgiving, present your requests to God.
~ Philippians 4:6

And pray in the Spirit on all occasions with all kinds of prayers and requests. With this in mind, be alert and always keep on praying for all the Lord's people. ~ Ephesians 6:18

Devote yourselves to prayer, being watchful and thankful.
~ Colossians 4:2

Dear friends, use your most holy faith to grow. Pray with the Holy Spirit's help. Remain in God's love as you look for the mercy of our Lord Jesus Christ to give you eternal life. ~ Jude 1:20-21

Lord, I pray that our home will be a reflection of our faith to all who enter. Help us to create a loving, peaceful home to return to each day. ~ In Jesus' Name.

Newlywed Book of Prayers

2 Our Marriage

May our union be kept strong by our willingness to
commit ourselves wholeheartedly
to God and to each other.

*"But at the beginning of creation God 'made them male and
female.''For this reason a man will leave his father and mother
and be united to his wife, and the two will become one flesh.' So
they are no longer two, but one flesh. Therefore what God has
joined together, let no one separate." ~ Mark 10:6-9*

Lord, I pray that our marriage would grow stronger with every
passing year. I pray that we would treat each other with mutual
love and respect. Help me to be the Spiritual Leader that my wife
needs. May I honor her, build her up, and support her as my wife.

Make us to be humble, gentle, and patient with one another. Make
us kind, compassionate, and forgiving. May our hearts remain loyal
to one another, forsaking all others. I pray that You create in us a
willingness to work together as a team; looking to You in all the
decisions that we make for our future. ~ In Jesus' Name.

*Wives, submit yourselves to your husbands, as is fitting in the Lord.
Husbands, love your wives and do not be harsh with them.*
~ Colossians 3:18-19

Be completely humble and gentle; be patient, bearing with one another in love. ~ Ephesians 3:2

Be kind and compassionate to one another, forgiving each other, just as in Christ God forgave you. ~ Ephesians 4:32

Marriage should be honored by all, and the marriage bed kept pure, for God will judge the adulterer and all the sexually immoral.
~ Hebrews 13:4

3 Our Communication
Let our communication be gentle,
encouraging and open.

A gentle answer turns away wrath, but a harsh word stirs up anger. ~ Proverbs 15:1

Lord, I pray for good communication between my wife and me. May we speak gentle not harsh words to each other. Help us to be conscious of what we say and how we say it, before we speak. May we seek to build up and encourage one another, not tear down. Help us not to assume the other knows and understands what we mean. Give us ears to hear, and help us to be slow to speak when we're angry. When confusion and misunderstanding occur, help us to communicate with love and forgiveness. ~ In Jesus' Name.

A wise man's heart guides his mouth, and his lips promote instruction. ~ Proverbs 16:23

Reckless words pierce like a sword, but the tongue of the wise brings healing. ~ Proverbs 12:18

Encourage one another and build each other up, just as in fact you are doing. ~ 1 Thessalonians 5:11

Newlywed Book of Prayers

4 Our Friendships

May our friends be like-minded
people of faith.

The righteous choose their friends carefully, but the way of the wicked leads them astray. ~ Proverbs 12:26

Lord, lead us to godly, like-minded couples to share our lives with. Help us make connections in our church. I pray that you give us wisdom in choosing friends. Protect us from any unwise ties. Help us to be the kind of people we are looking for in a friendship. I pray that you provide a strong Christian woman in my wife's life. One that will model dependence, integrity and faith in You.

~ In Jesus' Name.

Iron sharpens iron, so one man sharpens another.

~ Proverbs 27:17

Walk with the wise and become wise, for a companion of fools suffers harm. ~ Proverbs 13:20

Do not be misled: "Bad company corrupts good character."

~ 1Corinthians 15:33

Newlywed Book of Prayers

5 Our Church

May our church home be one we both love, a place where we can worship, serve, and grow in our faith. Make our church be one that is Bible believing and Spirit – filled.

I want them to be encouraged and knit together by strong ties of love. I want them to have complete confidence that they understand God's mysterious plan, which is Christ himself.
~ Colossians 2:2 NLT

Lord, I pray that we will make the attendance of church a priority. Not out of duty but because of our love for You and our desire to honor and worship You. I pray the establishment for our place of worship is mutually agreed upon. Lead us and guide us in setting a foundation before our children are born, so that we may grow in our faith and teach them together. ~ In Jesus' Name.

The human body has many parts, but the many parts make up one whole body. So it is with the body of Christ. ~ 1 Corinthians 12:12

Let the word of Christ richly dwell within you, with all wisdom teaching and admonishing one another with psalms and hymns and spiritual songs, singing with thankfulness in your hearts to God.
~ Colossians 3:16

Newlywed Book of Prayers

6 Our Children

May God give us children.
May He help us to nurture, love, and teach them the importance of knowing and serving Him.
Help us both be godly role models for our children.

Then God blessed them, saying, "Be fruitful and multiply."
~ Genesis 1:22 NLT

Lord, I pray that you would bless us with children. Help us to grow into Your likeness, that we may reflect and exemplify You to our children. May our hearts be full of Your Word so that we can help our children to know and understand Your ways at an early age. May You help us grow in them a love for You and Your Word, and give them a desire to serve You. ~ In Jesus' Name.

Teach them to your children, talking about them when you sit at home and when you walk along the road, when you lie down and when you get up. ~ Deuteronomy 11:19

Children are a heritage from the Lord, offspring a reward from him. ~ Psalm 127:3

Whatever you have learned or received or heard from me, or seen in me—put it into practice. And the God of peace will be with you.
~ Philippians 4:9

7 Her Spiritual Growth
May my wife grow in her faith.
May she walk in holiness and bear much fruit.

We continually ask God to fill you with the knowledge of his will through all the wisdom and understanding that the Spirit gives, so that you may live a life worthy of the Lord and please him in every way: bearing fruit in every good work, growing in the knowledge of God. ~ Colossians 1:9-10

Lord, I pray for my wife's spiritual growth. May You draw her to Yourself and give her a desire to know You more. May she find great delight and understanding reading and studying Your Word. Give her a heart that continually seeks after You. I pray she is holy as You are holy. (1 Peter 1:16)

Lord, I pray that my wife would be quick to forgive those who hurt her. Give her a tender heart that does not withhold forgiveness or bear grudges. May she be reminded of Your forgiveness toward her and live by that example. In addition, Lord, help her to grow in humility, asking for forgiveness when she offends another.

Lord, I pray that my wife would become a strong woman of prayer. Make her sensitive to the promptings of Your Holy Spirit. May she freely share her burdens with You. And when she does, may her faith grow as she sees Your faithfulness in answer to her prayers.

Lord, I pray that my wife would grow in the fruits of the Spirit.(Galatians 5:22-23) May love, joy, peace, patience, kindness, goodness, faithfulness, gentleness, and self-control, manifest in her as You continually mature her. I pray that my wife remains in You, so that her life bears much fruit for You. May she be reminded that apart from You, she can do nothing. ~ In Jesus' Name.

Therefore let us move beyond the elementary teachings about Christ and be taken forward to maturity. ~ Hebrews 6:1a

I am the vine; you are the branches. If you remain in me and I in you, you will bear much fruit; apart from me you can do nothing.
~ John 15:5

But grow in the grace and knowledge of our Lord and Savior Jesus Christ. To him be glory both now and forever! Amen.
~ 2 Peter 3:18

8 Her Influence

May my wife be a godly influence
and a holy example in her circles.

Whoever walks with the wise becomes wise, but the companion of fools will suffer harm. ~ Proverbs 13:20

Lord, I pray that You will make my wife to be a godly influence in church, at work, with family and whatever path You place her on. Give her a desire to fill her mind and heart with Your Word so that others see You and Your influence in her life. As people look to her, may she always lead them to look to You. May her walk not cause others to stumble, but may she live as a holy example that would draw others to You. May she also have a profound influence in the lives of our future children. Use her to teach them about You and Your great love for them. ~ In Jesus' Name.

Live such good lives among the pagans, that though they accuse you of doing wrong, they may see your good deeds and glorify God on the day He visits us. ~ 1Peter 2:12

Those who are wise will shine like the brightness of the heavens, and those who lead many to righteousness, like the stars forever and ever. ~ Daniel 12:3

Newlywed Book of Prayers

9 Her Work

May you bless my wife's work.
May she learn to depend on God
and glorify Him when she's successful.

Blessed is the one who does not walk in step with the wicked or stand in the way that sinners take or sit in the company of mockers, but whose delight is in the law of the Lord, and who meditates on his law day and night. That person is like a tree planted by streams of water, which yields its fruit in season and whose leaf does not wither—whatever they do prospers. ~ Psalm 1:1-3

Lord, I pray that You would bless the work of my wife's hands. Give her wisdom in all of her endeavors. May she acknowledge You, delight in, and live by Your Word. Protect her from any dishonest people and cause her to reject all wrong counsel. May she be like a healthy, fruitful tree which yields much fruit. May she honor You for prospering her though praise and giving generously according to Your Word. ~ In Jesus' Name.

"For I know the plans I have for you," declares the Lord, "plans to prosper you and not to harm you, plans to give you hope and a future." ~ Jeremiah 29:11

Honor the LORD with your wealth, with the first fruits of all your crops. ~ Proverbs 3:9

Whatever you do, work at it with all your heart, as working for the Lord, not for human masters, since you know that you will receive an inheritance from the Lord as a reward. It is the Lord Christ you are serving. ~ Colossians 3:23-24

10 Her Protection

May God protect my wife from all harm.
When danger or sickness comes near,
may God rescue her.

Though one may be overpowered, two can defend themselves.
A cord of three strands is not quickly broken. ~ Ecclesiastes 4:12

Lord, thank You that I am one with my wife and we are one in You. I pray that You would hear my prayers on her behalf. May she look to You as her rock, her fortress, and her deliverer. May she run to You for refuge and know that You are her strength. Help her sense that You are an ever present help in times of trouble. Your Word says, *"Because he loves me," says the Lord, "I will rescue him; I will protect him, for he acknowledges my name. He will call on me, and I will answer him; I will be with him in trouble, I will deliver him and honor him. With long life I will satisfy him and show him my salvation." ~ Psalm 91:14-16*

The LORD is my rock, my fortress and my deliverer; my God is my rock, in whom I take refuge, my shield and the horn of my salvation, my stronghold. ~Psalm 18:2

God is our refuge and strength, an ever-present help in trouble. Therefore we will not fear, though the earth give way and the mountains fall into the heart of the sea, though its waters roar and foam and the mountains quake with their surging. ~Psalm 46:1-3

Fear not, for I am with you; be not dismayed, for I am your God; I will strengthen you, I will help you, I will uphold you with my righteous right hand. ~ Isaiah 41:10

When you pass through the waters, I will be with you; and when you pass through the rivers, they will not sweep over you. When you walk through the fire, you will not be burned; the flames will not set you ablaze. ~ Isaiah 43:2

~In Jesus' Name

11 Her Temptation

May God help my wife
resist all temptation that comes her way.
May she see the way of escape and take it.

No temptation has overtaken you except what is common to mankind. And God is faithful; he will not let you be tempted beyond what you can bear. But when you are tempted, he will also provide a way out so that you can endure it. ~ 1 Corinthians 10:13

Lord, I pray You will protect my wife from all temptation and enable her to resist by calling on Your name. Please enable her to see the way of escape that You provide and take it. May the tactics of the enemy not ensnare her. Remind her of Your Word that's hidden in her heart. May she put on the full armor of God and use the offensive weapon of the sword, the Word of the Lord.

~ In Jesus' Name.

My son, do not forget my teaching, but keep my commands in your heart, for they will prolong your life many years and bring you peace and prosperity. ~ Proverbs 3:1-2

Marriage should be honored by all, and the marriage bed kept pure, for God will judge the adulterer and all the sexually immoral.
~ Hebrews 13:4

Finally, be strong in the Lord and in his mighty power. Put on the full armor of God, so that you can take your stand against the devil's schemes. For our struggle is not against flesh and blood, but against the rulers, against the authorities, against the powers of this dark world and against the spiritual forces of evil in the heavenly realms. Therefore put on the full armor of God, so that when the day of evil comes, you may be able to stand your ground, and after you have done everything, to stand. Stand firm then, with the belt of truth buckled around your waist, with the breastplate of righteousness in place, and with your feet fitted with the readiness that comes from the gospel of peace. In addition to all this, take up the shield of faith,with which you can extinguish all the flaming arrows of the evil one. Take the helmet of salvation and the sword of the Spirit, which is the word of God. ~ Ephesians 6:10-17

12 Her Integrity
May God help my wife
to walk in integrity all the days of her life.

For the Lord grants wisdom! From his mouth come knowledge and understanding. He grants a treasure of common sense to the honest. He is a shield to those who walk with integrity. He guards the paths of the just and protects those who are faithful to him.
~Proverbs 2:6-8

Lord, I pray for my wife to be a woman of integrity in everything she does. May everyone know her as a woman of her word, someone who is trustworthy and honest. I pray that you protect her reputation, and that she would always adhere to moral and ethical principles. ~ In Jesus' Name.

The man of integrity walks securely, but he who takes crooked paths will be found out. ~Proverbs 10:9

Do not lie to each other, since you have taken off your old self with its practices and have put on the new self, which is being renewed in knowledge in the image of its Creator. ~ Colossians 3:9-10

In everything set them an example by doing what is good. In your teaching show integrity, seriousness and soundness of speech that cannot be condemned, so that those who oppose you may be ashamed because they have nothing bad to say about us.

~ Titus 2:7-8

ABOUT THE AUTHOR

Doreen Wennberg is a Bible student and teacher and has been leading women's prayer groups since 1999. She is a wife and mother who attests to the power of prayer in countless ways.

She wrote the *Newlywed Book of Prayers, the Husband's version,* to help equip others on their new lifelong journey in marriage. The companion book *Newlywed Book of Prayers, the Wife's version,* is also available.

To Contact go to: www.doreenwennberg.com

www.ingramcontent.com/pod-product-compliance
Lightning Source LLC
Chambersburg PA
CBHW060648030426
42337CB00018B/3506